31 Years In The Desert

Castanita Fitzpatrick

All Things Beautiful Publishing

Milwaukee, Wisconsin

Castanita Fitzpatrick/All Things Beautiful Publishing
Street Address
P.O. Box 902
Milwaukee, Wisconsin 53201
getherwingsback.org

Ordering Information:
Quantity sales. Special discounts are available on quantity purchases by corporations, associations, and others. For details, contact the "Special Sales Department" at the address above.

31 Years In The Desert/Castanita Fitzpatrick
ISBN 9798667198024

Contents

Acknowledgements

A special thank you to Coach Misty who worked really hard with me on this book.
Also, to all the women who had everything to do with me being where I am today, from all the programs, agencies, probation, court judges, mentors, sponsors, friends and foes. I am grateful to have each of you being in my life.
With Daddie God blessing me with such amazing women in my life, you all have helped me become the woman I am today.
To the readers of this book, I pray that you see the desert storms of life can help you fly above all things and become the butterfly that lives in you. Nothing in life should hold you down. You must release it, forgive, and move on to your promise land.
Thank you to everyone, who has played a role on my journey.
Book two is on the way.
Castanita Fitzpatrick.

A Butterfly can only fly, if she uses the strength of her wings to break through!

–Castanita Fitzpatrick

CHAPTER 1

The Little Girl Within

For me, childhood wasn't easy. When I was five years old, I was molested by my mother's boyfriend. It was hard to tell her this, but as I laid in the bed, feeling like I needed her, I knew I had to tell her. She was drunk or high, I am not sure which one exactly, but I told her that her boyfriend had "played" with my private area. She didn't believe me, and she threw a shoe at my nose. Later she called my grandma and said, "I am sending your child to you." So, it was off to grandma's I went.

Living at grandma's turned out to be good, she made sure I always had the best of everything. My first bed was a brass headboard. She wanted me to have a nice bed, since my mom never provided for me. There was a window in the room, one day I looked out and saw a white pick-up truck and a man standing outside of it. I ran and told grandma, she later told me it was my father. He told my grandma to get me ready and he was coming back to get me.

Grandma got me ready the next day, pig-tails and all dressed up, hours passed, he never showed. No call, no nothing. This left me feeling that no one wanted me, neither of my parents wanted me. I was hurt and heartbroken. I went to a very dark place. I started living in the place that only lonely and abandoned children live. This is where I existed, and I was only five years old. I was drowning in sinking sand, without having the tools to pull my-self up.

CHAPTER 2

Sinking Sand

From there things only got worse. Grandma had always told me to go to school and be the best, yet I got caught up with the wrong crowd. I dropped out of school in the 6th grade and started using powder cocaine at the age of ten years old. I left school every day to go to the girl's house who got me started on this substance that made me escape reality. My reality within was non-existence, so I found an outward way to escape. There wasn't a day that went by where I didn't long to be with my mom. I was tortured by unanswered questions, where was she? Why didn't she love me? How did I end up like this? There were so many questions that went through my mind, leaving me feeling like I had done something wrong.

I couldn't understand why no one wanted me, when the reality of it was that someone *did* want me, I just couldn't see yet. My grandma was trying, yet I kept rebelling against everything she tried to do. I would sneak boys in when she was at work, destroy her house and clean up before she got home. This went on for a while until I found something else to get into. This type of behavior never stopped; it only got worse for me because I was seeking the attention that was missing in my life. I had no self-esteem at all. I was fat and ugly, and I never fit in with the kids on our block. When drugs took over my young life so did the life- style.

CHAPTER 3

A Walk Through Addiction

Soon, my drug use habit went through the roof. I would leave my grandma's house at night to be a part of whatever was going on, just to get that white powder that made me leave the reality of my so-called life. I remember going into a bathroom with this guy, he forced me to get on my knees, and said, "You're not a little girl anymore." Those words rang loud in my ears as the tears flowed down my face. He grabbed my head and pushed his penis in my mouth until it reached the back of my throat. I didn't know which hurt worse, the pain in the back of my throat or the painful fact that I was now a part of a world that I didn't understand.

My childhood was gone, playing outside became surviving outside, playing with dolls became playing with men to support my drug habit. Many times, as children, we are asked what do we want to be when we grow up? Unfortunately for me, that question was easily answered the day I put that demon in my nose. I knew if I wanted that white demon, I had to do what it had me to do to get it. The more involved I became with the white demon the more my life spiraled out of control.

Chapter 4

Family Secrets

When I was 11 years old, one-night Grandma and I were talking. She explained to me that she didn't want me sneaking out of the house, so I stopped sneaking out, and started doing drugs in the house. I also started sneaking boys into my room when she was asleep. Although, I wasn't having sex at this time, I was having oral sex so that I could supply my cocaine habit. Eventually I learned that my mom had her own demons as well. At the time all I knew was that her men were always more important to her than I was. My mom had her own demons she was dealing with. Which I had no clue what was going on with her. I knew that her men were always more important than I was. I can remember as a kid, while playing outside, seeing my friends in the neighborhood always have someone who cared about them and where they were. Everyday I could hear their family yelling for them to come inside, and I always wondered where my parents were.

Don't get me wrong, not every house on the block was great. I used to go down the street to my friend's house and play later to find out there were a lot of secret things that went on in that house. The men that lived there always tried to do things with me, but I wouldn't let them touch me down there. But, from time to time going through the kitchen to get to the bathroom was an adventure. I was too afraid to tell my grandma what was going on, although I believe she knew something, grandmas *always* know.

Chapter 5

Grandma's Wisdom

My interest in boys started at a very young age, around 8 years old. I had a crush on a couple of boys, but they never seemed very interested in me. Like the boy down the street, who was older than me or the boy with the cute eyes that everyone in the neighborhood liked.

Grandma did the best she could to keep me dressed in the styles most kids would wear, yet it didn't stop me from being teased, so going to school was something I wasn't interested in at all. When I did go, I would just leave and go home and bring boys by the house. Finally, after I really started getting out of control, grandma decided to move to a high rise building off the beach. It was so nice, it had a great view and a room of my own. Like I said, she always made sure I had the best in her eyes. I am glad she truly loved me.

Chapter 6

A Run Into The Desert

My grandma told me that my mom lived in Cleveland Ohio, and despite how much I knew that my grandma loved me, when she went to sleep, I left her house on the hunt to find my mom. I hitchhiked from Chicago to Cleveland, the highway I traveled was dark and scary, especially for an 11-year-old. Some of the truck drivers I came across were nice, some not so nice and sometimes I was left in places with no food, and no water, but the only thing that was on my mind was getting to Cleveland to find my mom. My heart was set on her loving me once she saw me. We would be a family and take care of each other. It was a nice thought, but unfortunately it never happened. State troopers picked me up and took me to a substation. They asked me what I was doing on the highway, I told them I was going to Cleveland to find my mom. By then I was somewhere in Ohio. They did an APB search for my mom. When she was found she came to the substation where I was, and she told the police that I wasn't her child and that they could do whatever they wanted to do with me. That hit me hard. It felt like she drove a nail through my heart and made me feel more worthless than I'd ever felt.

CHAPTER 7

Shackles & Chains

I was classified as a runaway and they took me to the detention center in Cleveland Ohio. Going back and forth to court mom made it clear to me that she didn't want me, and she made it known to the courts. At the detention center I served time and on our last court hearing my mom was told that she had to take care of me because I was her child. Back then CPS wasn't as strong as it is today. They placed me in her care and released me. I went to my mom's house where she was having a party and she told me that I couldn't stay there. So back to the streets I went, where I ended up getting rearrested.

Cleveland Ohio was the worst for me. I was raped by a man who had a disease and passed it to me. It scarred my tissues and worst of all it made me sick. I caught PID from him not taking care of his disease. I knew where my mother lived and went to her house. My body functions were shutting down. She told me it was my period. I was cramping so bad, and she made it clear that she didn't want me there and promptly left for work. I was pooping and peeing out of my mouth. One of my mom's neighbors found me wedged between the door and took me to the hospital. If I wasn't found when I was, I would have died. While in the hospital days past and my mom never visited me, until one day she and one of her boyfriends at that time showed up. They ate my lunch and as usual she fussed at me and called me worthless. I can recall feeling just like what she called me worthless. I never understood why she didn't love me nor want me. Still to this day I can't and will never bare children.

CHAPTER 8

High In The Desert

I finally got arrested again and this time they placed me in a runaway camp for teens far away from society. It was a coed; the boys were in one area and the girls were in another. I met a boy there who was older than me and we passed notes when we could. He was released from the teen center first, but he waited for me and we reconnected on the outside. I picked up where I left off with using. I would fight him to let me get high, he would let me and eventually he started getting high with me. Even though we got high together, he could stop, and I couldn't. I never had love before, and he gave it to me.

We stayed with one of his family members in the projects, I wanted to get high, so I took off on the ten-speed bike that was there. It was dark out and late, I was riding on the street then suddenly, this van came out of nowhere and hit me. The van didn't have any lights on, I ended up under the wheel of the van. The impact was so hard the bike flew one way, crushed into pieces, and the emergency team was trying to get me from under the tire. Thankfully, the only thing that was wrong with me was a broken leg. The young boy I was with later contacted my grandma in Chicago, and she came and got me. When we got back to her house, she made me feel as comfortable as possible despite the circumstances.

CHAPTER 9

Stuck In The Desert

Later, mom came from Cleveland and stayed with us. That didn't last long because she and I fought every day. I remember once, I was watching television and she came and took the remote out of my hand. We then exchanged words and it got physical. Grandma grabbed a hammer to get her off me and said, "Don't touch my baby." She told mom she couldn't stay there anymore. It was obvious that mom had been drinking, so she later left and moved down the street in an apartment with one of her men. I found out where she was and went to be with her. It was raining and I looked through the window and saw her, him and his daughter. I knocked on the door and they let me in, it was one of the most degrading feelings in my existence. After they let me in, I asked for something to eat because I had been out there for some time. Leaving grandma's house came naturally, so naturally that I would do anything to go out and be a part of the world that I had become accustomed to; including going into the bathroom and cutting my own cast off my leg.

CHAPTER 10

Grandma's Love

The boy I was in a relationship with went on for years. I would sneak him into my bedroom, against my grandma's wishes and hide him behind my bed. But eventually our relationship deteriorated, and he became something of my past. Even though we spent so much time together, I really don't remember much about him. Years later, we reconnected past and the only things that I know about him are what he has told me. A lot of my life is still a blur because I chose to block things out, the memories are just too painful. And those that I didn't block, seem to have been deleted by my drug and alcohol use.

I do, however, remember my grandma's love for me. I remember it was real, no one else's love was ever real. People lied to me and manipulated me just to get what they wanted, and I fell for it all the time. The thing is, they had what I needed, and they got what they wanted from me in exchange. Grandma's love was always real, yet I chased after someone who didn't want me, who never fed me, and who watched me sleep in an abandoned car while she went to work. Yet, I still wanted and needed her love and acceptance. I always felt that most kids had what I wanted even though I didn't know what was going on behind their doors. I just knew that they had a family; a mom and dad. And I wanted one too!

Chapter 11

Adulting

My teen years were the beginning of the worst, yet as my adult life started so did a lot of other activities that only made my life more complicated. I joined a door to door magazine sales crew. I got involved with the top salesperson and who was also involved in using crack cocaine. We were the idea couple to some. As our relationship grew, so did my need for being locked in the bathroom with him after we returned to the hotel from work. Later we decided to leave the magazine crew and go to his hometown. That was a big mistake on my part, I thought he really loved me. I didn't realize that the drugs were so powerful, and I was nothing in his territory. We stayed with his mom and he got a job with the local trash company.

His mom and I would talk about her son, she wasn't to be pleased with him and his being hooked on drugs. She also knew we would argue and fight. When he would go to work, I would walk about the town. It was very small, and everyone knew everyone. I felt alone and by myself even with his mom around.

At least, when I was on the sales crew it gave me the opportunity to have a place to stay, a way to travel, and another way to continue to get high. The bosses didn't condone it, yet they didn't mind having people who were addicted, had backgrounds, and didn't really have anyone. They knew they would go and make money just to support their habit. When the drug use was out of control, they would let the people go, send them back home if they had one, or leave them where we were. Granted I'm not saying anything bad about door to door sales crews, I'm just saying what happened to me when I was there.

Chapter 12

Chasing The White Ghost

Prostitution and drugs had become the beginning of no end for me. I would travel all over the United States just to get that white demon in my body. By this time in my life I had ventured to the next stage, from powder cocaine to now free base. Free base is a form of powder cooked up with baking soda. There weren't any chemicals in the powder. This was in the late 70's early 80's, when the pimps and pushers were strong and the girls that were under them were as weak as they came. I was one of them. I wanted that white ghost, and I did whatever it told me to do.

On the south-side of Chicago, there was an apartment, where you would knock on the door and if you didn't have any money you would have to go into the bathroom and perform oral sex with this guy whose penis was so huge it would choke out of you whatever you had in your system. But I did whatever the white ghost told me to do. I was there for days, not bathing and smoking, tricking, until the lady who owned the house told me that I had to go. Now, with nowhere to go I tried looking for my mom. I found out she was back in Chicago since grandma passed away. She and another one of her men friends had gotten yet another apartment on the north-side of Chicago. I went to find her only to find her working in the bar scene. I forgot how I came across the knowledge of where she was or who helped me find her. But I deeply regret it. What I thought would be a great mother and daughter relationship later came to be two people getting drunk and high together.

I went to bars with her, got high with her, but she told me I couldn't live with her. She put a lock on her icebox so I couldn't eat her food, put a lock on her phone so I wouldn't use it when she let me come by and bathe. She knew I was on the streets and she was the blame for it, yet she didn't want me to stay with her or be the mom that I needed in my life. She made me feel worthless, saying things to me so harsh, they could cut through a tough piece of meat that was cooked too long. One day she was having a get high party with her friends. I knocked on the door and she acted like she didn't know who I was. That was the last day I saw who I thought was my mom.

Chapter 13

Back To The Desert

After all the terrible events that took place with my mom, I went back to what I knew, the streets. Spun a cocoon around myself and indulged in the lifestyle that I knew; drugs, prostitution, and now more than ever, homelessness. Homelessness took me to places I wouldn't wish on my worst enemy. I traveled from city to city and state to state. There wasn't a city where I didn't blend in. Living with the worst of the worst, until I finally came to believe was the best. People of the homeless community became a family to me. I created this illusion that I had a family and I was just passing through. I would get high with them until my money ran out then I took to the hustling seen and did what I knew, prostitution. In most states I lived in I would get hooked up with the main dealer or the known man on the streets. This only made it worse for me because I couldn't control my crack habit. I continued using day in and day out never realizing my mind was gone, my life as I knew it was gone, I was totally in the state of just existing in the world.

When things would get rough for me, I would leave and find somewhere else, another city, or another state, only to continue the madness of the false realization that I was normal. Sometimes, I would stop the smoking and start drinking because that was what was going on with everyone at that time, yet I wanted to get that ghost back in my life. Some of the places I've been were horrible. I lived in the woods in Florida, where we would sleep in dome tents. There was a whole family in the woods, and the dope dealer in the trailer park. In New York I lived in a shelter and got hooked up with somebody there. The dope house was on the corner and getting high was more of a fight then a hustle. I lived in abandoned houses in New Orleans where I would take a bath with gallon milk jugs and poop outside in the whole in the porch. I learned how to do some of the most outlandish things.

The desert I lived in had no life, no light, just a dark and dreary feeling of non- existence. No matter which way I turned, no matter which way I wanted to go there was nothing. I felt like I was nothing. Drugs took me on many trips, but the desert was always the landing field. The people that would cross my path were just like vapors formed from the desert. It was like the desert created everything I thought I needed at the time I needed it. However, much I wanted to get out, however much I wanted to feel human, I did just the opposite. I had become someone that floated on the dusty sands of the desert for 31 years.

Chapter 14

Holes In My Soles

Crack and cocaine controlled my life. Whatever it told me to do; I did it, wherever it told me to go I went there. I never thought I would become what it had made me become. I just existed in life, not caring, not knowing who I was any longer. I was the substance of a state of mind that only people would see in movies. Prostitution was my job to support my habit. Getting high just to have men do whatever they wanted to me. I would just lay there and not exist while the act was going on. Sometimes I would cry because of the disgusting feeling I felt while I lay there. I walked around day in and day out in dirty clothes, and I wore eight pairs of socks because I didn't have any shoes. The shoes I did have I left in a hotel running from a trick after I took his car. Socks were the easiest thing for me to keep, and to have. When one of them got dirty I would just take a pair off and keep on going. All I had were the clothes on my back.

I prayed and prayed that Daddy God would help me because I couldn't do it on my own. I often wondered how life would have been for me if I had just not used drugs at all. Looking at the women everyday getting on the bus going to work or wherever they were going, I remember saying I wanted to live life; but instead I went back to the corner or the block to blend in with the people who I called family and turned another trick to get what I needed for that moment. It became a daily, nightly, hourly, and then minute by minute thing. This went on and on for years and I just didn't know how to get out of the mess that had me trapped. I was confined to a lifestyle of destruction.

Chapter 15

My Journey

As the months turned to years so did my journey of homelessness, prostitution and drug addiction. I traveled all over the United States, until the journey took a turn when I came to Dallas Texas. This is when the rapes, abuse, and drugs got really bad. Oh, don't let me forget to mention the arrests that started to happen. First it started with just a misdemeanor then they told me (the jailhouse lawyers which are the girls who have been in and out) don't get that third one. That really put some fear in me, but it didn't stop me from being on the streets of Dallas. Every night and day were spent selling my body, doing drugs and dodging the police. The police got to know me quickly, because I became something, I regretted, a known prostitute on the streets. Even when I got jumped, raped and then left for dead the police said," Oh she is just one of those prostitutes." I got jumped so bad one night after leaving the truck stop. The guy and his friends followed me to the hotel and watched me as I went in the room and scored. When I came out, they beat me bad, and tried to put me in the back of the trunk and drop my body in the trinity river. But God's Grace was with me that night. Once they left, I crawled to the maintenance guy's room, he raped me and told me I could stay only for a while then I would have to go.

I remember one of the police officers used to bring me food. Some of them were just as bad as the men I sold myself to. They wanted me to do them favors to keep me out of jail. After being raped by one of the police officers, I lost all respect for the people I thought were there to save me. After multiple arrests one of the police officers that knew me, said that I desired to live a better life. This was so true, yet I just didn't know how to stop using drugs. I thought the life I was living was normal and then it became my reality. I was just existing, and death became something I came to be okay with.

Doing time was becoming scary for me, yet that didn't stop me. I had gone to numerous drug treatment centers, including the one in the county jail. I had even gone to the state prison, only to get out and go right back to what I knew, drugs, prostitution, and homelessness. For weeks and then days I was up using and selling my body with no sleep. It had to be about twelve days in total. Finally, I decided to get behind the wheel of a car, only to realize that my body was going to shut down. I stopped by the dope house (where we would buy drugs) just to get one more piece of crack to help me stay awake. Once I left there, I got as far as the stop sign and fell asleep. I went through the stop sign and hit the utility pole which landed on top of the car. The engine was almost in my lap, I crawled to the back-passenger door and walked away unscratched.

Chapter 16

Finding Grace In The Desert

On August 6, 2010 they were doing a sweep, which is what the police call cleaning up the prostitutes on the streets. They ran my name on the computer and by now I was on the run. I should have had a blue warrant yet when they ran my name nothing came up. So, they took me down to where they would do some tests on me to be sure I was healthy with no diseases and all was good. I went in front of a judge who asked me if I want treatment or jail? I said treatment. They later came to me and said they were going to give me a break. I went to the treatment center for that weekend and on Monday, I went to court only to get sentenced. The judge told me something so profound because I explained to her that I wanted to try to find my mom. She told me that if I kept living in the past, I would never have a future.

While in treatment at TDCJ Behavior Modification Program, my counselor asked me if I was left-handed or right-handed? See in treatment they always want you to write a good-bye letter to your drug of choice, well I wasn't up to writing another good-bye letter. So, I told her I was right-handed. She asked me to write a letter to my mom using my left hand. I didn't understand it, she said don't try to spell anything correctly just let the pen flow. I did. She then told me that the little girl inside of me never had a voice. After the letter was written she sat an empty chair in front of me and the little girl read the letter to her mom. This started the process of forgiveness. See all along the way, good seeds were being planted in me and I never knew it. For those people I am so grateful.

In the treatment center, I would see the ladies leave and come back with bags in their hands. I asked them where they'd gone, and they said to a place that helps women. The name of the agency shall not be mentioned. I signed up and went. I felt out of place because I thought that if they knew that I was a homeless prostitute they would judge me. The day was filled with workshops, one in which you would go to this boutique and pick out a suit. The lady that ran the boutique came to me and asked what size I was. I didn't know tears flowed down my face. I didn't know anything about what bra size, what pant size I was or anything. I felt so out of place. I told her that I have always been a woman, but I just want to be a lady. She then came to me with this suit and said for me to go try it on. WOW, I can remember the feeling of having on a suit, my first suit ever. I looked in the mirror and said, "Now I am a lady."

Chapter 17

A Butterfly Gets Her Wings

I went back to the treatment center a different lady. See, that place that us ladies went to really prepares you, builds up your self-esteem, and for me mine was gone. I had very low self-esteem and didn't believe in myself. I Felt worthless. Months past and then the facility head guy came to me and told me I was going to be the facility coordinator. The center is peer driven where the clients run the place. The staff, groups, rules and all other things are for the clients to learn accountability, and how to hold each other accountable for their actions. There was also a chain of command, the Facility Coordinator is the one who is at the head. There one is a coordinator for the men and one for the women who brings all concerns to the staff, and vice versa. I asked why he picked me, and he told me that he wanted me to become the executioner. I didn't know what that word meant so I had to look it up, it led me to a word *execute* which means put out. I went back to him and told him of my finding, and he said, "Yes put out, everything you have been searching for is already inside of you, I just need you to know how to bring it out." On that day the light bulb went off and I was awakened to wanting to do more for myself, my life, and most of all to wanting to recover everything that I had lost.

After that day, I started taking life by the horns knowing that my thirty-one years in the desert had finally come to an end and the cocoon I lived in had now burst and this beautiful butterfly was born. Now that butterfly had to learn how to fly. Once I got released, I realized how scared I was, how nervous I was. I kept thinking back of the times where the winter in jail was safer than the summers out on the streets. They said to me "meeting makers make it." All I could remember is a dream I had the night before my release: I was on the train talking with my sponsor and all the streets I had ever traveled had come up street after street after street, passing faster and faster. She told me to keep calm and to stay on the train until the train stops and she would be there. I did what she said and at the end of the line she was there. Well that dream came to pass. I was on my way to a meeting that we are supposed to go to for addicts, and alcoholics, I called my sponsor and she was there when the train stopped.

CHAPTER 18

My Process

As I was released in the program it was a different experience and a new life. The court program had a judge who was over the program said something to me that no one ever said to me, she said she believed in me, also my probation office said the same thing. I was already on fire for what life has to offer, and I was up for the challenge. In the court program they were stricter with a lot of rules which I never had in the years of being on the streets. On the streets there wasn't no rules just life or death situations.

My cry for help that day was answered for me to live a life of worth, to live a life of growth, change and mostly how to love myself. This has become one of the most difficult obstacles in the new life I have been given. During it all I learned that Daddie God was directing me. He changed my heart, which changed my mind, which had changed me.

Going through this program there were different phases you had to complete, I did them all successfully. Receiving the completion certificates did something so profound inside of me. I had never received a certificate for anything, never had a reward, nor had accomplished nothing in my life. Those pieces of paper sparked up the fire that was already inside of me, they reassured the essence of me being someone, not the person I once was: homeless, drug addict, and prostitute. I took those labels off me. I was then and only then did I become a survivor, no longer a victim yet there was still much work to do.

Changing my mind set had to be unleashed not just sitting there in the air of space. The process had taken root and now I was allowing it to grow along side with myself. I had to stay in transitional houses, learning how to live life on the outside. One of the houses didn't work for me so I got in touch with my mentor who later lead me to the house in which I was writing to while I was in the treatment center. At her house she showed me what it was to be a DIVA, and during all that, I remember her telling me I'm not going to do the work for you, you must do it. Living at the house you must pay your way so we would work the ballpark, after our portion of rent is paid, she would give us an allowance.

My mentor who came and got me from the treatment center the day I was released, help me with a search for my mom. One of my judges told me if I quit living in the past, I would have a future. My mom had become an addiction to me. Chasing after her wanting to love me, chasing after wanting to be accepted. So, I chose the crowd of people to feel that void, drugs just numb my pain. Wanting to find my mom so bad, she told me that day I wasn't ready to find her, before she sentenced me. Well my mentor and her brother got on line and I remember the last address where my mom lived. They paid for the service and helped me with the letter to write to the lady I was hoping was my mom. The letter was to the point. A few days later she called me at the ballpark where I was working and told me she received a phone call for me. I asked her from who? She told me your mother tears flowed from my eyes she gave me the phone number. For the first time in 31 years I talked to my mom on the phone. We talked everyday after that. I still had a lot of work to do with the unrealistic expectations of my mom. This was a process all its own, yet I didn't know what was in store at the time. The letter my counselor had me to write that day forgiveness process of my mom was okay at the time because seeing her face to face was all I wanted. I wanted to tell her I loved her, and that I forgive her before she died, that I knew she didn't know how to love me, yet I still forgave her. So, a couple of years passed, and we made plans for her and my auntie to come to Texas. In meeting her I was okay with whether she excepted me or not. Meeting her was all I wanted to do, when I did tears flowed hard then I saw my auntie for the first time. Tears where all over the airport. People were passing us as my mentor said they just got reconnected. When she and I had our mommy and daughter time I was able to tell her, Mom I know you didn't know how to love me, but I forgive you and if there's anything I've done I want you to forgive me. Even though she wasn't the mom I had always wanted she still was one of my biggest supporters in all I did or tried to do. We built a relationship long distance.

Chapter 19

Reunited

I finally was reconnected with my family after being separated for 31 years. I later was reconnected to my Papa who has past away now. I was able to hear him play the piano and laugh. He came to Dallas to visit me for my birthday one year. He was 98 when he past. After visiting Chicago, I was also able to reconnect to my dad. He and I are still building our relationship. I told him dad I forgave you. He then told me he tried to come and get me that day when I was five years old. My mom put an order of protection on him. My dad only lived 20 minutes or so from where I was. He told me had she not done that I would not have had to go through all I went through because I would have been with him.

.

While working on the relationship with my mom, still in the transitional living house I was still learning how to live life on the outside. I learned how to ride the bus, schedule, balance my time, the lady that ran the transitional house truly taught me a lot. It was almost time for graduation of the court program and one of the ladies had signed up for this apartment program, I did the same. Later I was in my first apartment. I could remember praying for one day I would wake up in the middle of the night and go to my icebox and get a drink of water. For years all I had was eight pair of socks and a long t-shirt. Now all my prayers were being answered and still a lot of healing and work to do.

In this apartment the housing program they provided all the furniture and it was scary for me. I slept with all the lights on. I had never had my own place when the staff member brought me to the apartment, I went to open the door, he told welcome home. After he left, I got down on my knees and cried and said thank you Lord, thank you Lord. I was overwhelmed, over joyed, and most of all grateful. I had for years the fear of living in the dark. Even today it taken me a while to sleep without my television on and the lights off. I guess you can say freedom of learning that I am going to be okay, and I don't have to fear the terrors of the night.

Now here comes graduation, before that however, I got involved with a man that was in the rooms. I asked this guy for a ride home gave him a kiss on the jaw. I asked for a ride and he not only gave me one home, he gave me one in my life. He was my dream come true, so I thought. Our relationship was good he gave me everything I could want, all my first, also with that relationship came a lot of hurt, pain, betrayal, denial, and a false sense of love. I didn't realize my part I was blinded by the wonderful things, not the sickness of the man I had gotten involved with. One day he came to my house and told me he had relapsed and me trying to keep him I took him to the store brought him some smokes, feed him. I had no clue that day would lead to many more like that. I had no clue being new in recovery myself, I think he knew that. Our relationship wasn't the same after that day. I started getting smart recognizing the behaviors that I use to do, he was doing them. So, I use to keep money in my closest he stole it, I knew yet didn't say anything to him. He would give me money only to want me to go in my bank account and get it back or get him money after he spent his getting high. So, what I did I had a just in case account for him. Every time he gave me money, I put it in that account. Every time he wanted money from me, I would get it from that account which was his own money. We would go to church, he would leave me and go back to his house and use. We would have a great weekend and he would ruin it by using after he left me. I truly didn't know how to love him, plus I truly didn't even know this man. One of the girlfriends he had in the rooms warned me of his using, and how he acted with her, until she used with him. I didn't listen to here say, I thought I could fix him. I didn't know myself yet, nor did I love myself enough to be in this relationship. He asked me to marry him on Christmas day I said yes. Only then did things got worse for us. My feelings for him was fading, to scared to what he might do. I had lost myself in this twisted relationship, a part of me I never knew he had never put his hands on me, the verbal abuse was just as bad. One time he got angry and I thought he was going to hit me, it was over some money he gave me. The first time he ever gave me money reminded me of the tricks I used to have sex with. It took me a long time to get over the fear of getting into a man's car. I hid myself from him only to be found again. Even today we are still in contact, however the love that was there could never be. He went in many treatment centers for his own reason, got involved with another woman. How many he had I would never know. He played us both, going back and forth between us. When one didn't give him what he wanted he would go to the other one. Getting out of this relationship I found me for the first time. Well I'm still learning myself every day, started loving me, learning who I am, forgiving me which I am still trying to do. Even though we have contacted again I have set a boundary, after lying and saying I was in a relationship and getting married. That was a sick twisted way of trying to get him out of my soul. Finally, I can say with all the mess I've been through with him my heart is now in Daddie God's hands waiting for the right one He will give it to.

Graduation Day was January 24, 2012. Wow that day was special within itself. I was two years clean and sober a few months had past and then a letter came in the mail, released from all obligation of the Dallas County Courts. Yes, off probation. After years of probation violations, after years of back in, back out of the jails, institutions, after years of just existing in life, I was now a member of society, so I thought.

Even though the courts and probation released me society never releases you. I had a hard time finding work. One reason was I never had a job, no job experience. I had taken many classes and workshops on how to build my resume still work was hard to find. They tell you in the workshops to build the resume on the experience you have, so I did just that. All the experience I had from jail being a trustee, the experience I had when I work at the ballpark to pay for my stay at the transitional living house, well I was surprised to find out I did have enough experience to get a job.

Living at my first apartment still things did get rough. I was still in the relationship with the guy and the people thought I moved him in with me, I didn't but that was the rules. To many overnight visits, coming by too often, I didn't have the guts to tell him not to, afraid I would lose him. I was getting ready to lose my apartment with no where to go. Not only was I required to attend various meeting, I was in a program that helped me pay some of my bills. Mostly I was looking for a job of my own. I started working at a restaurant making tips, this was all new to me and learning how to live life was new as well. Even though everyone in my support network told me this man wasn't any good for me, I continued to see him. Being in the housing program they came to me one day and told me it was reported I had someone living with me and I had to move out. I was then forced to see him the man I dread seeing face to face. I got a taste of the addictive side of him when I moved in with him. Not even a day with him he left me home that night said he was going to watch the game, hours had passed no call, nothing. When he got home the next night, I prayed that God put that man to sleep like he did

Adam and I pack what I could carry and didn't look back.
With no where to go I went to the bank and got blessed with some unexpected money so I could go to an extended stay hotel. Then the job search started again I found a job at a telemarketing company which didn't last long. However, it helped pay my rent for about a month. Then started I am staying with people who took advantage of my situation. My jobs were back and forth. I worked at the treatment center which I was once a client for 2 years. Left and went back to it. I just couldn't find my happy place with the jobs I had for some reason. I knew my passion was to help people. No matter what I went through all the years of back and forth I remained sober.

CHAPTER 20

Deja-Vu

Each year of my sobriety came new lessons to be learned even so I remained teachable. Having to start over I went to another program to help me with an apartment. I didn't know what to expect. The place they had placed me in was an apartment I use to get high in and was homeless in. When the man opened the door, I looked around and then when we reached the bedroom it all came back to me. When I moved in I started cleaning in the corner where I had slept when I was homeless and use to use in this very apartment was a cross. I picked it up and then and only then did I realize that God had me here for a reason. I was in the belly of the whale you could say, because not only was I in the same apartment I was in the same neighborhood not long ago I was selling my body, getting high, and hustling to survive. If I didn't say anything people didn't know who I was all but one. It was getting hard to live there. Fears kept me not really sleeping at night, and in the morning when I went to work wondering if one of the people, I use to hang with would break in or worse come knocking on my door. I didn't have much recovery under me currently, however I did have God. I clung to that notion that someday this will be just as it is a part of my story. I only stayed here for a few months making plans to move yet again. Within this year I can recall moving about 11 times. Finally, I call one of my mentors she has a transitional living home. I explained my situation and she let me come, on moving day the dope dealer was picking up someone both I knew, and he said to me I didn't know you lived over here. I just looked at him and said I am moving. We loaded up everything and went to the storage place and there my belonging stayed for a few years. Having to reach out for help at this stage of my recovery was a hard pill to follow, however I was working at a restaurant and made the call. My mentor told me she had room at her advanced house. Here goes another lesson inside the lesson. She helped get a job closer to where I was, I had to walk the highway to get to the bus stop even in the rain, storms and hot, cold weather. I did it for a year and as time went on, I was feeling better about myself, until he found me. This was 2014 only 4 years clean and sober yet I remained just that. Striving to better myself and becoming a better me I was still trapped in the loneliness stage and wondering what he was doing. I couldn't get him out of my system no matter what I said out of my mouth my heart felt something totally different. I took me years to finally say enough just like I did with my addiction. I prayed for Daddie God to help me stop going around this mountain. Yes, I said earlier we are still in contact, for some reason my spirit just isn't comfortable with it. It's like when ever blessing start showing up in your life there goes the enemy trying to detour you. That's how I feel about him. Yet again I have blocked him out of my life. If it is Daddie God's plan for a man to be in my life he will come when I am ready.

I stayed at the transitional living house for a year working on getting my own place again. Saving, working, and remaining clean and sober. It was and still is hard to find an apartment with prostitution felony and a drug conviction on your record. So, I reached out to a private owner who gave me a chance. It was Daddie God's blessing. When I moved in, I was working at the Dallas Convention Center. There I was applying for a job at Amazon with gave me the opportunity to become a problem solver and working there for almost 2 years. I was having problems with my right knee. Earlier in years the car I was in took a toll on my knee. It really started to lock up on me, and by this time it was really getting hard to walk. At work one night I just collapsed, and I was rushed to the emergency ER by some coworkers. Come to find out I needed a full knee replacement. This is when things started to get so overwhelmed. After numbers of doctor's visits, surgery was dated for February 2018. Now I am living on the third floor, so I had to move somewhere on the first floor, having a felony conviction this was a hard task to do within itself.

As time went on for mom and me, we started to share each other's mornings. I was getting off work and she was getting up for work. So, on my way home we would share coffee and conversation. This was the beginning of our relationship for years. Well 2017 she was planning to come down to Texas for her birthday. I was so excited she gets to be at my house instead of me going to Chicago to be at hers. It truly was a good feeling to know my mom was coming, did I have unrealistic expectations yes, I did, however all that changed when she got here. Mom was one who never helped me with anything and if she did, she would tell you about what she did, or make you feel like crap afterwards. So, what I did was just the opposite I didn't want her to spend any money on me when she came, I had all her favorites ready for her, she Googled the restaurant and meal she wanted, the state fair was in town so that was on the list to do as well. This time was going to be different then the first time she came. I didn't ask anyone for rides, or anything we took the bus, and surprising she was okay with that. It was going to be just me and mom. Well October came and mom arrived I went to the airport to pick her up and everything was great. We arrived at my house got her settled and her birthday began. I was shocked that she didn't do her normal self, fusing and telling me what I should do to my apartment, she really liked it. As the weekend went on everything, she wanted to do we did, food fun, the fair, rest, and movies, everything I had always wanted mommy and me time to be. Finally, when we talked, she said something so profound it really made my heart fall, she told me she was proud of me and that she loved me. For years I waited to hear those words from her, and I finally got them. I love her so much. Mom was leaving soon so we got her ready she slept well in my bed, I covered her up and kissed her on her forehead and told her goodnight. For years I had always wanted this moment, if I would have let things that hindered me in the beginning stop me and brought me back to where I was, I would have never had this blessing. Thank You Daddie God.

Mom went home and we did our usual coffee and mom and me time. It was November on a Sunday 12th I was off work for medical reason, and I was cooking. Mom was teaching me how to cook long distance. That was another thing we did together, loved it. Well we text instead of talked that day, mom finally go her a real phone. She had the very first boast mobile phone with an antenna. Well during our conversations, I was praying with mom and I told her she must move on from her past. Forgive all the men that hurt you. Mom was grieving still as well Papa my grandfather had past away two years ago. Mom didn't know how to process this. Her job was failing because of her mouth. Mom had to talk about everyone, I told mom please stop talking about people. Finally, they let her go. She didn't know anything but work. I prayed for her and her soul asking God to heal her, and I released mom to God.

Well we finished cooking and said our good-byes for the night. I didn't know that was the last time I would have talked with her. Come Monday morning I called her as usual, no answer, this was weird because even if she went to the store in the morning, she would have text me to tell me. I called and called and no answer, I had this sicken feeling in my stomach and something wasn't right, until I heard that still voice, I took her last night, not once but three times did I hear this. Panic came over me and I lost my breathe and didn't know how to take this. So, I called her building maintenance guy and had them do a wellness check, called my auntie and had her to go over to mom's house. She was found dead on the bathroom floor. I called my sponsor and friend to come to my house I totally lost it. For years I wanted mom to be in my life and for only five I had her.

Having so much to do yet the pain of feeling lost, and losing mom was the worst thing I could be dealing with. Knowing everything the programs taught me kicked in when I got to mom's house. I went in the bathroom laid on the floor and let out a cry that no one could every understand. I can't explain in words the cry sound I let out. Laying on the floor where mom's body was found holding the blanket, they wrapped her in was only the beginning of the pain of what I was having to face. I started getting everything packed up. My auntie mom's closest sister, I have another auntie as well they weren't that close. Mom was very bitter and angry, I will never know what was going on with her, nor will I know all she endured in her life to make her that way. Auntie told me when she walked in mom's house it was life, she got everything ready for her to find paper work, and documents and everything was laid out. I didn't want to know how mom died my guess was stroke or she committed suicide. Mom was still grieving Papa and the lost of her job sent her over the edge. What ever happen Daddie God has her now and that's all that matters.

Going to pack mom's things I just took control and all the skills I knew from everything I learned kicked in. I packed, rearranged, organized, and made phone calls. I didn't want to sell mom's things instead I found a women's shelter in Chicago that helps women get on their feet and get their own homes. So, my auntie's husband who is very understanding loaded up his van and we took her things there. Mom was a hoarder this woman had stuff everywhere. I mean she had more shoes, wow did she have shoes, shoes in three different closets. I continue to pack and get things done. I had only four days to get all done because I had to get back to Dallas and get ready for my knee replacement and get moved. I was very overwhelmed, yet I didn't show it. I had to be strong for my auntie who just lost her sister, and friend.

They had a special yet weird sister-hood, kind of like Thelma and Louise. That's what I called them. When they would call me and tell me about one another I would laugh and say okay Thelma or okay Louise pending on which one I am talking to. Auntie misses her shopping bubby. For days end she wouldn't show it yet she's grieving her own way. Being strong for her is all I knew to do, and deep down inside I was broken, hurt, and numb at the same time. I really didn't know how to feel. I masked it even today. Today it's hard and I have my mommy moments where calling her to help me cook, have our coffee in the morning. I just start saying out loud "good cup of coffee mommie."

CHAPTER 21

A Butterfly Gets Her Wings Back

As mom's house was getting emptied out here came the time for us to go the funeral pallor and view the body. I went in and they had my girl on gurney I went back where she was, and that loud cry came out again and I bent over and kisses her cold still body and told her I loved her. I touched her had and told her mom I love you. She was so cold lifeless however her head was tilted to face me like she knew I was looking at her. I can't get that vision out of my head. That was yet one of what I was up to face, the next thing was going to the city hall and picking up her death certificate, then after the viewing of her body, her friends, co-workers and family came and paid their respects, I had to complete shutting down her existence. I called agencies, companies, insurances place, this place, that place, and finally it came to go home. I had to pick up her ashes and get my girl back to Dallas with me.

When I made it back to Dallas the time spent with my auntie, we started to build our relationship. She is my biggest supporter, as well my other auntie. Dealing with mom's death has taken a toll on me. I guess you can say I still haven't grieved as much as I should, however mom is in heaven and Daddie God has given me another angel. It's been now two years since her passing. I took mom's ashes, and set her free by the still waters.

Getting back was a task because I had to get ready for surgery, and get moved at the same time. Because I have a felony conviction of prostitution and drugs, no one wanted to rent to me. Well I had to get moved by December, and my surgery was in February. I searched and searched for a place, and finally the last place I came to they looked my record up there in the office, the property manager was in the office, the cooperate manager was there, and they both told me don't disappoint me go get your money orders. I did just that. Leaving the condo, I was comfortable in got moved, and got the surgery done. Did that stop all the hurt and pain I was feeling, no it didn't I was up against a financial battle, a battle of self, a battle of despair, however I stayed faithful to Daddie God who has provided, He kept me through it all. No matter what society throws at me, I stood strong, no matter what job I lost, I stood strong, no matter how less money I have am standing on His promises, that He will provide all my needs. See Daddie God took the disease of addiction, He took the old sight I had, and gave me a new pair of glasses, see Daddie God gave me a new knew to walk tall and strong. No matter what society throws at me I still stand.

After the surgery the process of learning to walk again was scary. My doctor made sure I had the best care possible. Once all was done, I went through a season of people pleasing in my life. Then I had to get ready for yet another obstacle which a blessing was around the corner. I started studying for my drivers license because people were getting tired of taking me places. So, I did just that and before long I got it, then Daddie God blessed me with my first vehicle. I was going to school using my credits I got from being in jail. Stopped for a while because I didn't have my GED nor diploma. Yet Daddie God blessed me with the right people at the right time in my life. I speak so many places and I was speaking at a conference and the teaches there wanted to give me that blessing. See all I wanted to do was to walk across the stage and get my high school diploma, one of the teachers there found a school in Fort Worth that home schooled me and now I have my high school diploma. There are so many women that I am grateful for. Because of these women I am becoming the woman Daddie God wants me to be.

I have gone through much since August 6, 2010, I have accomplished a lot as well. 31 years in the desert at 9 years clean and sober, that's my 40 years in the wildness, now I have seen my red sea parted before me, I seen my enemies defeated, I walked around Jericho silently in prayer, now today I embrace the journey of learning how to fly into my promise land.

I didn't use any names in my book, however if you're reading this, just know how grateful I am for all you have done, said and continue to do from your heart. You all have taught me how to love me, believe in me, and brought me out of the desert.

ABOUT THE AUTHOR

Castanita Fitzpatrick is a living testimony of Gods love, grace, and redemption. She has overcome molestation, drug addiction, homelessness, and prostitution. Castanita resides in Dallas, Texas where as a Motivational Speaker, as she empowers women to recover, and overcome the struggles of addiction, and life struggles. She is also the founder of "A Butterfly Gets Her Wings Back" where she does outreach Ministry in prisons, women's shelters, as well as giving back to her community.

For more information visit getherwingsback.org

Made in the USA
Columbia, SC
15 May 2023

16483918R00039